Annick Vincent, MD

My Brain Needs

Living with Hyperactivity

Translated from the French version by
Heidi S. Hoff

LES ÉDITIONS
Quebecor

Bibliothèque et Archives nationales du Québec and Library and Archives Canada cataloguing in publication

Vincent, Annick, 1965-

My brain needs glasses

(Collection Psychologie)
Translation of: Mon cerveau a besoin de lunettes.
For children.

ISBN 978-2-7640-1660-2

1. Attention-deficit hyperactivity disorder - Juvenile literature. 2. Attention-deficit hyperactivity disorder - Juvenile fiction. I. Title. II. Series: Collection Psychologie (Éditions Quebecor).

RJ506.H9V5513 2010   j618.92'8589   C2010-941790-9

Translator: Heidi S. Hoff
Editor: Jacques Simard
Graphic designer: Marianne Tremblay
Proofreader: Jennifer Makarewicz
Illustrator : Mathieu Guérard

Legal deposit: 2010
National Library of Quebec
National Library of Canada

Original edition published in 2004 by Académie Impact, Québec (Canada), under the title « Mon cerveau a besoin de lunettes. Vivre avec l'hyperactivité ».

All rights reserved under International Conventions.

© 2010, Les Éditions Quebecor,
une compagnie de Quebecor Média
7, chemin Bates
Montréal (Québec) Canada
H2V 4V7

All translation, publishing, printing, representation and adaptation rights, in total or in part, are reserved in all countries. The reproduction of any extract of this book by any means, whether electronically or mechanically, especially by photocopy or microfilm, is strictly prohibited without written authorization from the publisher.

Les Éditions Quebecor receives support for their publishing program from the Société de développement des entreprises culturelles (SODEC, Agency for the Development of Cultural Enterprises).

Government of Québec — Tax credit program for book publishing — Gestion SODEC

We acknowledge the financial support of the Government of Canada through the Book Publishing Industry Development Program (BPIDP) for our publishing activities.

DISTRIBUTORS:

• Canada and United States:

MESSAGERIES ADP*
2315, rue de la Province
Longueuil, Québec J4G 1G4
Tél.: (450) 640-1237
Télécopieur: (450) 674-6237
* une division du Groupe Sogides inc.,
filiale du Groupe Livre Quebecor Média inc.

• France:

INTERFORUM editis
Immeuble Paryseine, 3, Allée de la Seine
94854 Ivry CEDEX
Tél. : 33 (0) 4 49 59 11 56/91
Télécopieur: 33 (0) 1 49 59 11 33

Service commande France Métropolitaine
Tél. : 33 (0) 2 38 32 71 00
Télécopieur: 33 (0) 2 38 32 71 28
Internet: www.interforum.fr

Service commandes Export – DOM-TOM
Télécopieur: 33 (0) 2 38 32 78 86
Internet: www.interforum.fr
Courriel: cdes-export@interforum.fr

• Suisse:

INTERFORUM editis SUISSE
Case postale 69 – CH 1701 Fribourg – Suisse
Tél. : 41 (0) 26 460 80 60
Télécopieur: 41 (0) 26 460 80 68
Internet: www.interforumsuisse.ch
Courriel: office@interforumsuisse.ch

Distributeur: OLF S.A.
ZI. 3, Corminboeuf
Case postale 1061 – CH 1701 Fribourg – Suisse

Commandes: Tél. : 41 (0) 26 467 53 33
Télécopieur: 41 (0) 26 467 54 66
Internet: www.olf.ch / Courriel: information@olf.ch

• Belgique/Luxembourg:

INTERFORUM BENELUX S.A.
Fond Jean-Pâques, 6
B-1348 Louvain-La-Neuve
Tél.: 00 32 10 42 03 20
Télécopieur: 00 32 10 41 20 24

Preface

Attention-Deficit/Hyperactivity Disorder (AD/HD) is a problem that is becoming better and better known. As a result, one sometimes gets the impression that it is more and more common. The need to inform oneself on the subject has thus increased considerably in the last few years — a need that has been filled for parents, teachers and mental health professionals by numerous publications. However, even though children are among those who have the greatest need for information on the subject, very few truly informative and useful books for kids with AD/HD have been published (and not a single one in French, until this book, in the original French).

Fortunately, Annick Vincent has filled that gap with My Brain Needs Glasses. Now, not only children with AD/HD, but all kids can be adequately informed. They can finally understand why their friends, their classmates or they themselves act or react as they do.

Annick Vincent is an excellent psychiatrist devoted to helping adults with AD/HD. She is also a sensitive woman and a mother who is a good listener for her children. She was thus the perfect person to undertake such a task. My Brain Needs Glasses is a book for which children have been waiting for a long time. Their patience will be well rewarded by this simultaneously simple and complete text. A text that I would like to have written. Thank you, Annick.

Guy Falardeau
Pediatrician

Preface
of the Second Edition

Imagine for a minute that you are a little boy or a little girl affected by attention-deficit/hyperactivity disorder (phew!), more commonly known as AD/HD in health and education circles. It's a problem that you would have a hard time naming, let alone understanding. Toward whom or what do you turn to understand what is happening to you?

Adults (parents, teachers, educators, doctors...) all have access to a wide array of information about this neurodevelopmental disorder thanks to the publications, television and radio programs, conferences and the Internet. However, children have very few high-quality information resources designed just for them.

My Brain Needs Glasses is precisely the "gift resource" so very much needed by children seeking answers to their questions. In visually attractive packaging and with a simple language that nonetheless preserves scientific rigor, Annick Vincent, mother and psychiatrist, has given us a book exceptional for its appropriate tone and content. The story of Tom told here can thus be put in the little hands of our children, but also those of parents, teachers, educators, doctors ... in short, in the hands of anyone who already has some knowledge of the subject, as well as those who would like to learn about it!

Good reading!

Johanne Piché
Pediatric psychiatrist

Comments from adults with AD/HD

I remember, when I was little, I was called scatterbrained and a chatterbox.

In spite of my parents' help, it was very hard to study. I was spacy, impulsive and slow. I had trouble getting organized. I was thought lazy. I felt inferior to others and threatened by failure at school. In spite of everything, I loved to learn.

Thirty-four years separate me from Tom. If I had had the same luck that he did, I would have been more successful in school and had a more harmonious social life, a career I liked and, consequently, better self-esteem.

Now, I'm taking care of myself. My love of learning is still there and now I'm more enthusiastic. Now that I'm better equipped, life seems more promising to me.

Catherine Ripoche

As a child, I was like Tom. School was a nightmare that gave me stomachaches. Nonetheless, thanks to my parents' support and my little creative and perfectionist side, I made it through all the stages up through university. However, I turned in my work late and filled with errors caused by distraction. The result: I was always stressed and convinced that the "motor of my car" (that is, my brain) was not up to the task.

Since then, I have learned what the trouble was and now I put on "glasses." I no longer have the impression of wandering in a maze. I'm cruising on the highway with a good "car." I'm successful in my work. I'm proud of what I've accomplished and I don't want my son, who has the same problems as I do, to go through the same sort of questioning that cast a shadow over my youth.

Fortunately, he is lucky by being surrounded by people that understand the nature of his difficulties quite well. With his "glasses," he's doing well now. He uses the tips and techniques that he is given, he concentrates better and retains the notions learned in class better. He also has better self-esteem.

Today, my only regret is that I didn't wear "glasses" when I was Tom's age. How lucky he is!

Carole Bilodeau

Acknowledgments

A very special thank you to the adults and children affected by AD/HD who, by sharing their experiences and their strategies for adapting to this neurological disorder with us, have permitted us to better understand their difficulties and to better intervene with appropriate treatments.

Thank you to the mental health professionals in the field, the parents, teachers, health professionals and researchers for their constant efforts to grasp the complexity of this disorder better and to find individualized treatments.

A thank you from the bottom of my heart to all those who participated from close by or from far away in the development of this book: to my family and friends, to my patients and colleagues, to the students, parents and personnel at École Les Sources. Your contributions, your support and your enthusiasm for this project allowed it to take shape and to become what it is now.

Thank you also to the readers — with hopes that their curiosity and their interest in better understanding AD/HD is contagious! Good reading!

Annick Vincent
Psychiatrist

Hello, my name's **TOM**. I'm **8** years old and I'm in third grade. This is my family.

I go to school. These are my friends and my teacher.

Ever since I was little, I've had a tendency to "space out" —my mind wanders easily. Ideas jostle in my head like BUMPER CARS. I'm distracted by noises, but also by my own thoughts.

I've tried hard, but I make careless mistakes, I forget my lunch box and I've lost lots and lots of BASEBALL CAPS...

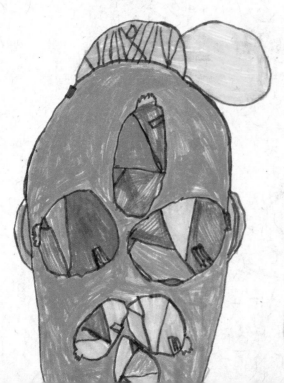

My parents  and my teacher have to help me. Often, I get exasperated and, sometimes, I get angry. It seems like my brain has a hard time getting going, which means that I often get started at the last minute. After that, things go pretty well, but then I'm distracted by the next thing I think about. My efforts are scattered and I have a hard time finishing what I start. I've really tried, but I can't help it!

I feel as if my brain has lost its **band leader**. I forget the passing of time. I read, but I have a hard time remembering the details of the story. I have to start over and over again.

Noises distract me—people call me a **WEATHERVANE** because I'm always turning every which way. It's frustrating because, even if I put all my energy into it, I still have a hard time getting organized. One day, another boy said that I must be stupid or lazy. That really hurt.

My parents say that I was a real **tornado** when I was little. Even as a baby, I couldn't stay in one place. My mother laughs when she says that I learned to run before I learned to walk.

Thing's have gotta move!

My TEACHER has often given me warnings because I talk in class. Even if the subject is interesting, I can't manage to sit still in my chair—I move and talk non-stop. When I have an idea, I have to say it right away. This bothers my friends, but it's really hard for me to control.

Most of the time, I'm funny and imaginative. My friends laugh when I clown around. I have a lot of good ideas. I'm known for my ability to find original solutions when problems arise. I'm full of projects all the time. But I don't have any brakes. In the schoolyard, I run all over the place. I've been given warning cards because I bump and push the other kids too much as I go flying by.

Sometimes, I lose control. My emotions become like a big wave and I throw a fit.But, I'm not mean...

It's as if the

BATTERIES

in my brain were

supercharged...

It's tiring in the long run.
Some evenings, I can't even
fall asleep. I move around non-stop.
Lots of ideas dance in my head. I want to sleep,
but I just can't do it.

My parents, totally exhausted, have tried stories, massages, even threats, but nothing

works. In the morning , on the other hand, I have a hard time getting going. My mother and father have to drag me out of bed…

Being distracted and fidgety is sometimes a dangerous mixture. I can be pretty clumsy. In spite of my best efforts, I frequently hurt myself and make messes.

My grandmother
says that my mother
was just like me when
she was little. She was
a space cadet 🌙, and
ran and climbed all over just
like me. She had new cuts
and bruises every day.

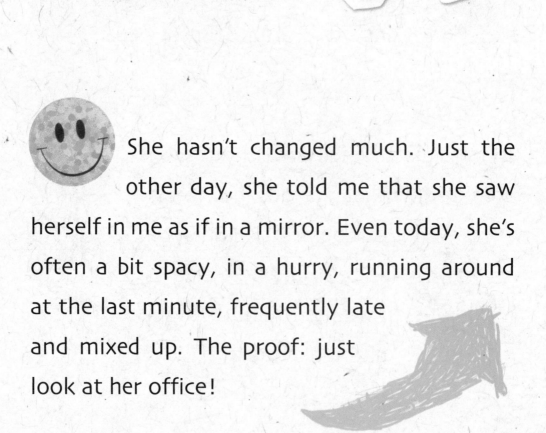

She hasn't changed much. Just the
other day, she told me that she saw
herself in me as if in a mirror. Even today, she's
often a bit spacy, in a hurry, running around
at the last minute, frequently late
and mixed up. The proof: just
look at her office!

Mom's office

Last year, my teacher, who knew other kids with similar problems, suggested that my parents consult a specialist to understand what was happening to me.

We went to see a doctor.

He explained to us that he thought I had

Attention-Deficit/Hyperactivity Disorder,

or simply

It's a problem that happens when the brain has

a hard time focusing its attention or putting on

the brakes when it should.

For a message to get to the brain, it has to be transported on wires called **neurons.** The information traffic

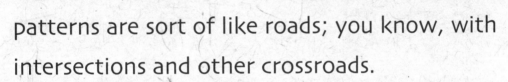

patterns are sort of like roads; you know, with intersections and other crossroads.

Normally the messages know where to go and the traffic police—**the neurotransmitters**—make sure that they start and stop at the right times, and that they yield the right of way when they should.

Summary of AD/HD

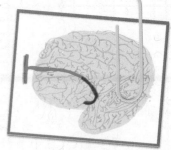

Individuals affected by AD/HD have at least six symptoms of inattention and/or six symptoms of hyperactivity, repeatedly (at least often) and non-adaptively, and not comparable to the level that is developmentally normal for their age. Here are the criteria to look for:

1. Inattention

☐ Has difficulty paying attention to details or makes careless mistakes.

☐ Has a hard time maintaining attention.

☐ Seems to not listen when spoken to directly.

☐ Doesn't follow instructions and doesn't finish his tasks (without showing antagonistic behavior).

☐ Has difficulty in planning and organizing his work or activities.

☐ Avoids certain tasks or does them grudgingly, especially if they require a sustained mental effort.

☐ Loses things that are necessary for his work or activities.

☐ Is easily distracted by external stimuli.

☐ Frequently forgets things in daily life.

2. Hyperactivity and Impulsiveness

MOTOR HYPERACTIVITY

☐ Fidgets with hands and feet or squirms in chair.

☐ Gets up in class or in other situations where one should stay seated.

☐ Runs about or climbs excessively (with increasing age: feeling of restlessness or fidgetiness).

☐ Has a hard time keeping still at school or in recreational activities.

☐ Is "on the go" or acts as if "driven by a motor".

☐ Talks too much.

IMPULSIVENESS

☐ Blurts out answers before the questions have been completed.

☐ Has difficulty waiting his turn.

☐ Interrupts or intrudes upon others.

To make a diagnosis of AD/HD in a child or adult, all of the following characteristics should be present:

☒ Showed some symptoms before the age of 7 years.

☒ Has certain functional handicaps caused by the symptoms that occur in at least two different settings (home, school, work, etc.).

☒ Is significantly affected in several parts of his life (social, school, professional, etc.).

☒ The symptoms have lasted more than six months and are not explainable by another mental or emotional condition (for example, anxiety).

AD/HD with predominant attention deficit = corresponds only to the criteria in list 1.
AD/HD with predominant hyperactivity = corresponds only to the criteria in list 2.
Combined AD/HD = corresponds to the criteria in lists 1 and 2 (the most common form).

Adapted from the *Diagnostic and Statistical Manual of Mental Disorders*, Fourth Edition (DSM-IV), American Psychiatric Association, Washington DC, 1994.

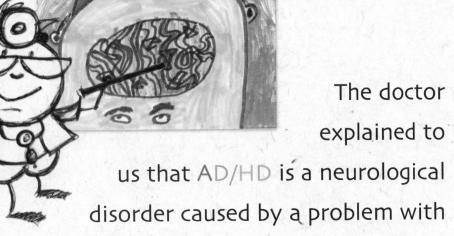

The doctor explained to us that AD/HD is a neurological disorder caused by a problem with the INFORMATION HIGHWAYS in the brain. When the TRAFFIC POLICE aren't effective (for example, when they don't see clearly), the traffic becomes snarled, and then it's a real mess. The ideas get all mixed up and bump into each other.

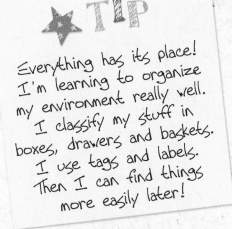

⭐ TIP

Everything has its place! I'm learning to organize my environment really well. I classify my stuff in boxes, drawers and baskets. I use tags and labels. Then I can find things more easily later!

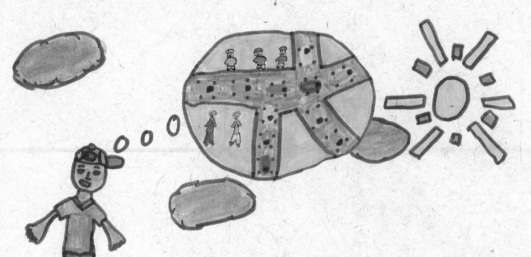

Priorities change depending on which idea manages to get to the head of the pack. Movements become less controlled, the fidgets set in. Talking and gestures are rushed, waiting isn't possible anymore, everything is urgent. Even emotions can overflow. AD/HD is a problem of BEiNG ABLE To— not of WANTiNG To.

I learned that there are treatments available that can help me correct the symptoms of AD/HD . They give the traffic police on the information highways better vision, a little like glasses for the brain.

When the brain wants to concentrate on one thing, the traffic police need to keep other commands (other ideas, actions and words) from pushing forward. The police put up road blocks.

 TIP

I'm finding tools to help me remember important information. I draw or I write down the things I don't want to forget in a notebook or I post messages on my bulletin board.

 In my case, AD/HD makes it seem as if all the commands come at the same time.

So, my ideas, my actions and my words are less coordinated and more impulsive.

When I make a big effort, I manage to activate some of the traffic police, but not always enough or for a very long time.

TIP

Every time I'm faced with a task, I take the following steps:

1) I break the task down into shorter little steps.
2) I do the most important steps first.
3) I give myself reasonable deadlines to respect.
4) I congratulate myself when I succeed. I give myself rewards when I can (for example, more time for an activity I like).

The doctor told us that AD/HD is often hereditary. So it's transmitted in our **genetic baggage** that comes from our parents, like the **color of our eyes** or our **hair**. Some children will develop it because their brain was damaged when they were little (for example, because they were premature or they had an infection, like meningitis). AD/HD affects boys and girls.

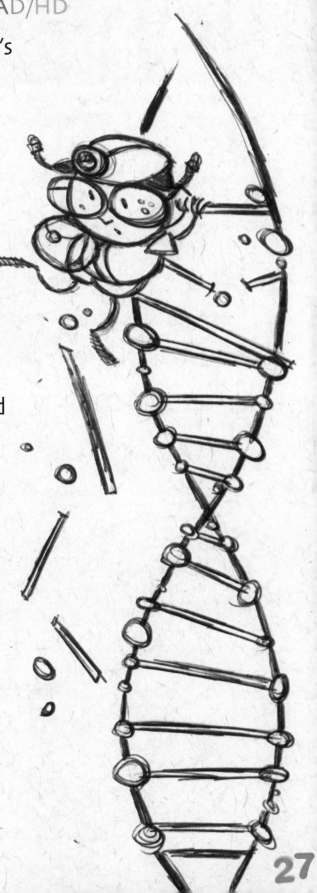

In our immediate family, my mother and I are affected. According to the doctor, certain people only have the attention problems and others just have the fidgets. But most of the time, the children and adults affected by AD/HD have a combination of all three:

«COMBO *inattentive·fidgety·impulsive*».

Hmmm... I think I'll take the combo!

COMBO AD/HD
...
INATTENTIVE
FIDGETY
IMPULSIVE

My parents were surprised to learn that almost half of the children with AD/HD will continue to have some related problems as they grow up, and even as adults. That means that, even if my mother is all grown up, her brain still needs glasses.

My genetic baggage

It's important to treat AD/HD because it can cause difficulties at school (or at work for adults), at home and with friends. Some kids have so much trouble at school that they drop out. Others are so impulsive that they aren't able to follow instructions. Sometimes, kids with AD/HD hurt themselves or have accidents. On the other hand, having lots of original ideas and projects is quite an advantage when it's well channeled. There are plenty of champion athletes and heads of companies who have AD/HD and have learned to master it.

When I learned
that I had this
problem, I
was sad. I felt
different from
my friends.
But at the
same time,

I was happy
to finally learn what was happening
to me. I understood that I wasn't stupid, like
that other boy said.
My brain works
differently, that's all!

★ TIP

Tidal wave of emotions in
sight? I don't hesitate to
take a little break to relax
and loosen up. I will feel
better taking a step back
instead of letting myself be
overwhelmed by emotions.

☺ TIP

"Know yourself!"
I watch myself and try to
figure out the conditions
that I work best in.
In silence?
With soft music?
While sketching?

I explained to my friends that I'm made this way, that's all! I'm a little like my friend Julia, who couldn't see the board well anymore and squinted her eyes until it got to the point where she needed to wear glasses. The difference is that no one sees my glasses!

You know, a lot of people, like me, are able to function with AD/HD, but it takes lots of effort.

In spite of everything, some people don't succeed as well as they could. Others get discouraged, criticize themselves and become more and more stressed out.

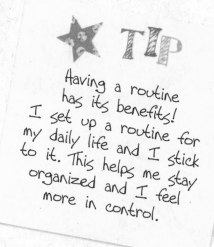

★ TIP

Having a routine has its benefits! I set up a routine for my daily life and I stick to it. This helps me stay organized and I feel more in control.

For my part, I was lucky to learn about my problems early enough and to have found solutions for them. Now I have glasses for my brain and they look great on me!

Hmmm.. Very interesting!

The first step is definitely to know what AD/HD is. My parents and I have read books about it and we've even found some interesting web sites on the Internet.

But be careful! You have to use common sense while reading about it and not believe everything that is written. My parents made me realize that it's worth the effort to check on the source of information…

to be sure that no one fools me.

TIP

I'm getting organized! Color codes, lists, memos, calendars and note cards all help me remember important tasks. That way I can get organized more efficiently.

My *parents*, my *teacher* and *I* have learned to *work as a team* to help me stay organized. They're like my coaches.

They help me by stimulating me to get started, to hold my interest and to stay concentrated. When I get scatterbrained, they remind me what the instructions are. They also help me to use my calendar well. I discovered that by using memos and putting everything in its place I get less confused.

35

I learned to break down tasks into **smaller pieces** and I have fewer last minute rushes. I play **Sports** to channel my energy and I try to control myself when I'm about to interrupt someone. This takes enormous **effort.**

When I let go, I lose my concentration. It's as if I take away my brain's glasses.

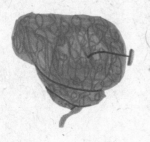

TIP

I move, you move, he moves...

I channel my need to move into exercise and sports. I feel less restless the rest of the time.

• • •

Waste my time? No way! I've equipped myself with devices for measuring time: a watch, an alarm clock, an hourglass...

Also, I now have
a watch with an
     alarm setting.
          I use it to make sure I
          start or finish on time.

I still have moments when I don't
have control of my ideas and
actions. In addition,
waves of emotion are
never far from the
horizon. But I try to
     use self-control and it's big
      job every day. Whatever
     happens, crying or getting
     mad is not the answer.

37

The doctor explained to us that, often, you need to take medication to help the brain with AD/HD work better.

These medications work like tiny glasses inside the body and directly improve the work of the traffic police.

Some of these medications have short-term effects. In this case, you need to take them many times a day. Others can be taken in the morning and work all day. We need to find the right type and adjust the dose, because everyone is different.

Sometimes the medications produce effects that we don't want, that are called SECONDARY EFFECTS or side effects (for example, lack of appetite or difficulty falling asleep). We have to visit our doctor regularly, because he's the person who can help us find a good medication.

For ME, it took almost three months. For my MOTHER, it took longer, because the first medication that she tried didn't help her. I have a FRIEND who also has AD/HD but he doesn't take any medication.

I think that the important thing is to know that my brain needs glasses and to use all the "glasses" that suit me. My parents and my teacher help me get organized.

I do my best to apply myself and my medication makes it easier for the traffic police in my brain to do their work.

It still embarrasses me when people ask questions about AD/HD. I don't like it when people don't understand or when they make fun of me.

TIP

Solve a problem? No problem!
Here are some useful steps toward solving problems:

1 I define the problem.

2 I make a list of possible solutions.

3 I choose a solution.

4 I apply the chosen solution.

5 I evaluate the impacts of that solution.

6 If necessary, I redo the process by choosing another solution.

At the beginning, I thought I was the only one with this problem. But my doctor told me that about **one *in twenty*** kids has AD/HD. That means that at my school, there is probably one child per class who is affected.

In a movie theater seating *200*, that means about *10* people. And in a region with *200,000* residents, that means *10,000* people!

★TIP

I surround myself with positive people who help me.

I highlight my accomplishments.

I'm proud of who I am and what I do.

That also means that there are lots of people who have the same problem as I do! Fortunately, they can find solutions that work for them.

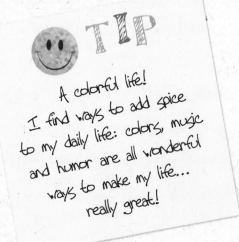

TIP

A colorful life!
I find ways to add spice to my daily life: colors, music and humor are all wonderful ways to make my life... really great!

And you? Are you affected by AD/HD? If not, you might know other children, adolescents or adults who are. I hope that my story will help you to understand them better.

Until next time!

I'm going to go play my journal is finished!

Also available from the same author

My Brain STILL Needs Glasses - ADHD in Adults
Les Éditions Québec-Livres, 2013

ADHD manifests itself during childhood with symptoms of inattention, hyperactivity and/or impulsivity. The methods used to reduce the symptoms act like glasses for the brain, by helping concentration or curbing fidgetiness. More than half of the children with AD/HD will still manifest symptoms in adulthood. Thus, they STILL need glasses and can benefit from knowing what tools are available to them as grown-ups.

Along with humorous insights and lively testimonials, the reader will discover the clinical symptoms, the scientific literature and the pharmacological treatments available to treat this neurological problem. This guide also offers a host of effective tips and practical hints specifically designed to help affected adults — and those around them — live with ADHD in their daily lives.

Resources and references

INTERNET RESOURCES

As with all research on the Web, we advise you to verify the credibility of the sources of the information. Here are some interesting sites:

ww.aacap.org
American Academy of Child & Adolescent Psychiatry

www.aap.org
American Academy of Pediatrics

www.add.org
Attention Deficit Disorder Association (ADDA)

www.addvance.com
Answers to your questions about ADD (ADHD) by Patricia O. Quinn, M.D. and Kathleen Nadeau, Ph. D.

www.addwarehouse.com
A.D.D. Warehouse, on-line catalog of AD/HD resources

www.aqeta.qc.ca
Learning Disabilities Association of Quebec (LDAQ)

www.associationpanda.qc.ca
Parents Able to Negotiate AD/HD

www.caddac.ca
Center for ADD/ADHD Advocacy, Canada

www.caddra.ca
Canadian ADHD Resource Alliance

www.chadd.org
Children and Adults with Attention Deficit/ Hyperactivity Disorder

www.ldac-taac.ca
Learning Disabilities Association of Canada

www.ldanatl.org
Learning Disabilities Association of America

www.myadhd.com
Provides rating scales and history forms that can be electronically transmitted, and over 100 treatment tools for use in your home, school, or pratice

www.nichcy.org
National Dissemination Center for Children with Disabilities

www.ordrepsy.qc.ca
Ordre des psychologues du Québec

Consult Dr Annick Vincent's website for other suggestions, tools, books and links to many AD/HD support groups around the world.

www.attentiondeficit-info.com

BOOKS ABOUT ADHD

Barkley, R. A. (2000). *Taking Charge of ADHD: The Complete Authoritative Guide for Parents.* New York: Guilford Press.

Bertin, M. (2011) *The Family ADHD Solution: A Scientific Approach to Maximizing Your Child's Attention and Minimizing Parental Stress.* New York: Palgrave Macmillan.

Gordon, M. (1992). *I Would If I Could.* DeWitt, NY: GSI Publications.

Hallowell, E. M., and Ratey, J. J. (1995). *Driven to Distraction: Recognizing and Coping with Attention Deficit Disorder from Childhood through Adulthood.* New York: Simon & Schuster.

Handelman, K. (2011) *Attention Difference Disorder: How to Turn Your ADHD Child or Teen's Differences into Strengths in 7 Simple Steps.* New York: Morgan James Publishing.

Jensen, P. S. (2004). *Making the System Work for your Child with ADHD.* New York: Guilford Press.

Moulton Sarkis, S. (2008) *Making the Grades with ADD, A Student's Guide to Succeeding in College with Attention Deficit Disorder.* Oakland: New Harbinger Publications, Inc.

Nadeau, K. G., Littman, E. B., and Quinn, P. (1999). *Understanding Girls with AD/HD.* Silver Spring: Advantage Books.

Nadeau, K.G. (2006). *Survival Guide for College Students with ADHD or LD.* Washington, DC: Magination Press.

Nadeau, K. (1998). *Help4ADD@High School.* Silver Spring: Advantage Books.

Phelan, T. W. (2003). *1-2-3 Magic.* Glen Ellyn, Illinois: ParentMagic Inc.

Quinn, P.O., Ratey, N.A., Maitland, T.L. (2000). *Coaching College Students with AD/HD, Issues and Answers.* Washington D.C.: Advantage Books.

Vincent, A. (2010). *Mon cerveau a besoin de lunettes: Vivre avec l'hyperactivité.* Montréal, Les Éditions Quebecor.

Vincent, A. (2010). *Mon cerveau a ENCORE besoin de lunettes: Vivre avec l'hyperactivité.* Montréal, Les Éditions Quebecor.

Vincent, A. (2013). *My Brain STILL Needs Glasses: Living with Hyperactivity.* Montréal: Les Éditions Québec-Livres.

TIPS

Tips, tricks, and more tips… To help you remember all the tips that Tom suggested in his journal, here is a summary that you can cut out and keep with you.

Everything has its place. Learn to organize your environment well. Sort and put away your stuff in boxes, drawers or baskets. Use tags and labels. You'll be able to find your things more easily afterward!

• • •

Find tools to help you remember important information. Draw or write down the things you don't want to forget in a notebook or pin them on a bulletin board.

• • •

Avoid getting scatterbrained! Every time you have to do a task, take the following steps: 1) break down the task into shorter little steps; 2) do the most important steps first; 3) give yourself reasonable deadlines and stick to them; 4) congratulate yourself when you succeed and give yourself rewards when you can (for example, more time for an activity that you love).

• • •

Know yourself! Watch yourself and try to find the conditions in which you work best. In silence? With soft music? While sketching?

• • •

Tidal wave of emotions in sight? Don't hesitate to take a little break to relax and loosen up. You will feel better taking a step back instead of letting yourself be overwhelmed by emotions.

Having a routine has its benefits! Set up a routine for your daily life and stick to it. This will help you to stay organized and you'll feel more in control.

•••

Let's get organized! Color codes, lists, memos, calendars and note cards will all help you to remember important tasks. That way you'll get organized more efficiently.

•••

I move, you move, he moves... Channel your need to move by doing exercises and practicing sports. You'll feel less restless the rest of the time.

•••

Waste your time? No way! Equip yourself with devices for measuring time: a watch, an alarm clock, an hourglass...

•••

Solve a problem? No problem!
Here are some useful steps toward solving problems:
1. Define the problem.
2. Make a list of possible solutions.
3. Choose a solution.
4. Apply the chosen solution.
5. Evaluate the impacts of that solution.
6. If necessary, redo the process by choosing another solution.

•••

Surround yourself with positive people who help you. Highlight your accomplishments. Be proud of who you are and what you do.

•••

 A colorful life! Find ways to add spice to your daily life: colors, music and humor are all wonderful ways to make your life... really great!